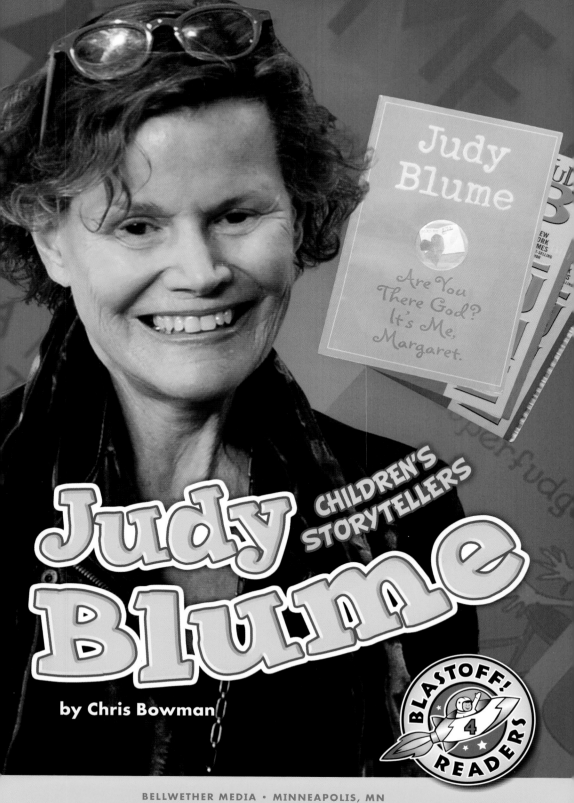

CHILDREN'S STORYTELLERS

Judy Blume

by Chris Bowman

BELLWETHER MEDIA • MINNEAPOLIS, MN

Note to Librarians, Teachers, and Parents:

Blastoff! Readers are carefully developed by literacy experts and combine standards-based content with developmentally appropriate text.

Level 1 provides the most support through repetition of high-frequency words, light text, predictable sentence patterns, and strong visual support.

Level 2 offers early readers a bit more challenge through varied simple sentences, increased text load, and less repetition of high-frequency words.

Level 3 advances early-fluent readers toward fluency through increased text and concept load, less reliance on visuals, longer sentences, and more literary language.

Level 4 builds reading stamina by providing more text per page, increased use of punctuation, greater variation in sentence patterns, and increasingly challenging vocabulary.

Level 5 encourages children to move from "learning to read" to "reading to learn" by providing even more text, varied writing styles, and less familiar topics.

Whichever book is right for your reader, Blastoff! Readers are the perfect books to build confidence and encourage a love of reading that will last a lifetime!

This edition first published in 2016 by Bellwether Media, Inc.

No part of this publication may be reproduced in whole or in part without written permission of the publisher. For information regarding permission, write to Bellwether Media, Inc., Attention: Permissions Department, 5357 Penn Avenue South, Minneapolis, MN 55419.

Library of Congress Cataloging-in-Publication Data

Bowman, Chris, 1990-
  Judy Blume / by Chris Bowman.
    pages cm. – (Blastoff! Readers: Children's Storytellers)
  Summary: "Simple text and full-color photographs introduce readers to Judy Blume. Developed by literacy experts for students in kindergarten through third grade"– Provided by publisher.
  Includes bibliographical references and index.
  Audience: Ages 5-8
  Audience: K to grade 3
  ISBN 978-1-62617-268-5 (hardcover: alk. paper)
  1. Blume, Judy–Juvenile literature. 2. Authors, American–20th century–Biography–Juvenile literature. 3. Children's literature–Authorship–Juvenile literature. I. Title.
  PS3552.L843Z56 2016
  813'.54–dc23
  [B]
                              2015000861

Printed in the United States of America, North Mankato, MN.

Table of Contents

Who Is Judy Blume?

Judy Blume has been an award-winning author for more than 40 years. She has written nearly 30 books for children, teens, and adults.

Readers love her stories for their honesty about growing up. More than 85 million copies of her books have been sold worldwide!

An Active Imagination

Judy was born in Elizabeth, New Jersey, on February 12, 1938. She lived with her parents and older brother, David.

"I worry that kids today don't have enough time to just sit and daydream."
Judy Blume

N
W E
S

Elizabeth, New Jersey

As a young girl, Judy was shy and small
for her age. Other kids teased her and she
felt like she did not fit in. Judy **distracted**
herself by daydreaming. She made up
stories while she played with her toys.

Reading was also a source of comfort for Judy. She liked checking books out from the library. She often spent her **allowance** at the local bookstore.

When she was 9 years old, Judy's family moved to Miami Beach, Florida. There, she began to open up. She enjoyed singing, painting, and roller-skating. She also continued coming up with stories.

! **fun fact**
Judy's favorite books were the *Betsy-Tacy* series by Maud Hart Lovelace.

A New Dream

Judy's family soon moved back to New Jersey, where she attended junior high and high school. Then in college, she studied to become a teacher.

During this time, Judy fell in love with a young lawyer named John Blume. They got married before Judy's senior year of college. Soon, they had a son and a daughter. After graduation, Judy stayed home to care for them.

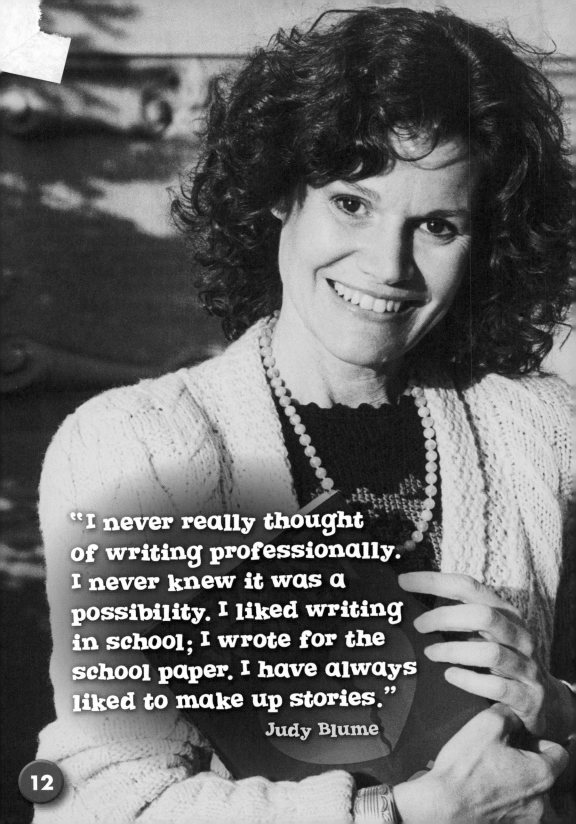

"I never really thought of writing professionally. I never knew it was a possibility. I liked writing in school; I wrote for the school paper. I have always liked to make up stories."

Judy Blume

Judy loved raising her children. But she felt like something was missing. She began writing books for kids. Many people doubted Judy, including her husband. Nobody wanted to **publish** her stories.

Eventually, she took a **creative writing** class. Judy's teacher helped her improve her writing. She believed that Judy could be a successful author. Soon her first book was published!

! fun fact
At first, Judy planned to draw the pictures for her books.

Judy's first two books received mixed **reviews**. But she knew that she could do better. Within a year, *Are You There God? It's Me, Margaret* was published. It was a hit! Kids loved reading this **realistic** story about growing up.

SELECTED WORKS

Are You There, God? It's Me, Margaret (1970)

Then Again, Maybe I Won't (1971)

Freckle Juice (1971)

Tales of a Fourth Grade Nothing (1972)

Otherwise Known As Sheila the Great (1972)

Blubber (1974)

Superfudge (1980)

The Pain and the Great One (1984)

Fudge-a-Mania (1990)

Double Fudge (2002)

Judy continued writing books based on
real-life experiences. Readers liked her
stories because they could connect to
her characters.

Many of Judy's books focus on the troubles of getting older. She writes about **themes** such as bullies, new schools, loneliness, and friendship. She also covers family issues like divorce and **sibling rivalry**.

! fun fact

Judy based her character Fudge on her son when he was young.

Her books do not always have happy endings. But Judy lets readers know that it is okay to be confused about growing up.

Another common theme in Judy's books is **puberty**. She writes from the **perspectives** of both boys and girls as their bodies change.

POP CULTURE CONNECTION

Judy's novel *Tiger Eyes* made its way to theaters in 2013. It was directed by Judy's son. It was her first movie shown in theaters!

BASED ON THE BESTSELLER BY
JUDY BLUME

TIGER EYES

IN THEATERS THIS SUMMER

"A good writer is always a people watcher."
Judy Blume

Not everyone has liked how she writes
about difficult topics. Some people have
even tried to ban her books! She is one of
the most commonly **censored** authors in
the United States. But this honesty is also
why her books are so popular.

The Lessons Continue

Judy has no plans to stop writing any time soon. She is currently working on her next **novel**. Meanwhile, her books continue to teach readers that experiencing changes is all part of growing up.

IMPORTANT DATES

1938: Judy Blume is born in New Jersey on February 12.

1969: *The One in the Middle Is the Green Kangaroo* is published.

1970: *Are You There God? It's Me, Margaret* is named a *New York Times* Outstanding Book of the Year.

1983: Judy receives the Eleanor Roosevelt Humanitarian Award for her work against censoring.

1996: The American Library Association gives Judy the Margaret A. Edwards Award for lifetime achievement.

2000: Judy receives the Library of Congress Living Legend award.

2004: National Book Foundation presents Judy with the Medal for Distinguished Contribution to American Letters.

2012: National Public Radio names *Forever* one of the 100 Best-Ever Teen Novels.

2012: *Scholastic Parent & Child* magazine names two of Judy's novels to its 100 Greatest Books for Kids list.

Glossary

allowance—money given to a person on a regular basis

censored—removed or changed because something is considered dangerous or upsetting

creative writing—the study of how to write stories and poems

distracted—took one's attention away from something or someone

novel—a longer written story, usually about made-up characters and events

perspectives—points of view

puberty—the time of change when a person's body grows into adulthood

publish—to print someone's work for a public audience

realistic—like real life

reviews—articles that discuss the quality of something

sibling rivalry—fighting between brothers and sisters

themes—important ideas or messages

To Learn More

AT THE LIBRARY

Blume, Judy. *Tales of a Fourth Grade Nothing.* New York, N.Y.: Puffin Books, 2003.

Nault, Jennifer. *Judy Blume.* New York, N.Y.: AV2 by Weigl, 2013.

Wheeler, Jill C. *Judy Blume.* Edina, Minn.: ABDO Pub., 2005.

ON THE WEB

Learning more about Judy Blume is as easy as 1, 2, 3.

1. Go to www.factsurfer.com.

2. Enter "Judy Blume" into the search box.

3. Click the "Surf" button and you will see a list of related web sites.

With factsurfer.com, finding more information is just a click away.

Index

The images in this book are reproduced through the courtesy of: Patrick McMullan Co./ Sipa USA/ Newscom, front cover, p. 4; Bellwether Media, front cover (books, background), all interior backgrounds, pp. 9, 14, 16-17, 21; LHB Photo/ Alamy, pp. 4-5; Jonathan Skow/ Corbis, pp. 6-7; Lucy Nicholson/ Corbis, pp. 8-9, 20; kritskaya, p. 10 (rings); Brian A Jackson, p. 10 (books); Joan Neary/ Corbis, pp. 10-11; J. Smestad/ Corbis, pp. 12-13; Kucher Serhii, p. 13; Romain Blanquart/ MCT/ Newscom, pp. 16-17; AF Archive/ Alamy, p. 18; krtkidselements009881/ Newscom, pp. 18-19.